ALL AGES WELCOME

*Recruiting and Retaining Younger Generations
for Library Boards, Friends Groups, and Foundations*

A **UNITED FOR LIBRARIES** ACTION PLANNER

LINA BERTINELLI
MADELINE JARVIS
KATHY KOSINSKI
TESS WILSON

CHICAGO / 2020

ALA Neal-Schuman purchases fund advocacy, awareness,
and accreditation programs for library professionals worldwide.

LINA BERTINELLI is the workforce librarian at the Enoch Pratt Free Library and Maryland State Library Resource Center in Baltimore, MD. She has a BA in linguistics from the University of Arizona and an MLIS degree from Drexel University.

MADELINE JARVIS is the adult and information services manager at the Marion (IA) Public Library. She earned a BA in sustainable community development from Northland College and an MLIS degree from the University of Iowa.

KATHY KOSINSKI is the member services and outreach manager at Califa Group. She has a BA in English and Spanish language literature from the University of Michigan's College of Literature, Science, and the Arts, and an MS degree in information from the University of Michigan's School of Information.

TESS WILSON is the community engagement coordinator for the National Network of Libraries of Medicine, Middle Atlantic Region. She earned a BA in English from Washburn University, an MFA in creative writing from Chatham University, and an MLIS degree from the University of Pittsburgh.

© 2020 by the American Library Association

Extensive effort has gone into ensuring the reliability of the information in this book; however, the publisher makes no warranty, express or implied, with respect to the material contained herein.

ISBNs
978-0-8389-4742-5 (paper)
978-0-8389-4790-6 (PDF)

Library of Congress Control Number: 2020007037

Book design by Kim Thornton in the Tisa Pro and Rift typefaces.

♾ This paper meets the requirements of ANSI/NISO Z39.48-1992 (Permanence of Paper).

Printed in the United States of America

24 23 22 21 20   5 4 3 2 1

United for Libraries: The Association of Library Trustees, Advocates, Friends and Foundations, is a division of the American Library Association with approximately 4,000 personal and group members representing hundreds of thousands of library supporters. United for Libraries supports those who govern, promote, advocate, and fundraise for libraries, and brings together library Trustees, advocates, Friends, and Foundations into a partnership that creates a powerful force for libraries in the 21st century.

www.ala.org/united

We dedicate this book to our mentorship parents, David and Veronda.
Thank you for all you have done for us!

Contents

Change Is Here and Will Be Here Again / vii

Generational Differences
(and What We Have in Common)

1

The ABCs of Recruitment and Retention

4

Defining and Managing Diversity
for Your Advocacy Group

24

Onboarding: Tried and True Practices

26

Fundraising with the Debt Generations

40

Conclusion: Assess, Adapt, Attract / 45

Additional Resources / 47

Change Is Here and Will Be Here Again

> Millennials in America are more likely to have visited a public library in the past year than any other adult generation.
>
> —Abigail Geiger, Pew Research Center

WE ARE IN THE MIDST OF TURBULENT DEMOGRAPHIC CHANGE. IN 2017, Millennials (born between 1981 and 1996) surpassed Baby Boomers (born between 1946 and 1964) as the largest generation in the workforce,[1] and in 2019 they surpassed Baby Boomers as the largest generation overall.[2] Not to be outdone, by 2028 Generation X (born between 1965 and 1980) will also have greater numbers than the Boomers.[3] After decades of omnipresence, Boomers are losing ground, and it is time for library boards, Friends groups, and foundations to look at recruiting younger generations. This is an easy enough statement to make, yet recruiting young members is an issue that has plagued library advocacy groups since the days when Boomers *were* the young members.

This book will focus mainly on the recruitment, management, and fundraising of Millennials because they are the next generational powerhouse in terms of numbers and tend to be the focus of current research on generational differences. This focus is not to discount the other two "younger" generations. The oft-ignored Generation X is steadily gaining presence in library board makeup and has long served as the bridge between Baby Boomers and Millennials.[4] The yet-unnamed Generation Z or Post-Millennial crowd (starting from 1997) is voting, in college, and/or entering the workforce with optimism and a tenacious drive for change. All three generations need to be considered important in your advocacy work and cannot be forgotten. We have created this book to provide tips, tricks, and best practices that are blendable across the generations.

NOTES

1. Richard Fry, "Millennials Are the Largest Generation in the U.S. Labor Force," Pew Research Center, April 11, 2018, www.pewresearch.org/fact-tank/2018/04/11/millennials-largest-generation-us-labor-force/.
2. Richard Fry, "Millennials Projected to Overtake Baby Boomers as America's Largest Generation," Pew Research Center, March 1, 2018, www.pewresearch.org/fact-tank/2018/03/01/millennials-overtake-baby-boomers.
3. Fry, "Millennials Projected to Overtake Baby Boomers."
4. Lina Bertinelli, Madeline Jarvis, Kathy Kosinski, and Tess Wilson, "Beyond Using the Library: Engaging Millennials as Civic Library Leaders" (poster presented at the American Library Association Annual Conference, New Orleans, LA, June 2018), https://drive.google.com/file/d/1AdqBPpJowmHSLOUzvsXnbc0zG2jSr-Ek/view.

Generational Differences (and What We Have in Common)

AS MILLENNIALS HAVE ENTERED THE WORKFORCE, THERE HAVE BEEN numerous conversations about managing the differences that mark this generation. However, when it comes to volunteering, motivations are similar across all generations. In 2018, United for Libraries surveyed 866 library trustees, Friends, and foundation members and asked how they were recruited to their board or other advocacy group. The majority of millennial respondents indicated that they joined the group for the same reasons as older generations: a willingness to serve, excitement about their community, and a love of libraries and reading.[1] Other industries have come to the same conclusion. Nicholas Tejeda, CEO of the Hospitals of Providence Trans-Mountain Campus, started a millennial advisory group and found that "there are a lot of things Millennials care about just as much as any other generation did, such as that the organization has a noble vision and it's based on serving a community."[2] Respondents across all generations are also motivated by their children. According to a report by the Corporation for National and Community Service, almost 40 percent of parents volunteer across the United States and contribute services worth $15.2 billion.[3]

Where differences do exist is in how Millennials discover volunteer opportunities and the time they have to commit to them. In the United for Libraries survey, less than half of millennial respondents learned of service opportunities through word of mouth, compared to 62–63 percent of respondents in all other generations. Older generations have had more years to cultivate personal networks, while Millennials might have spent the past few years building a family, getting an education, or moving between jobs, and could have missed opportunities to form the connections that word-of-mouth systems rely on.

According to the survey, meeting logistics proved to be a possible barrier for millennial participants who wanted to serve on boards. One respondent captured the importance of this with the statement: "Volunteer board service can be difficult to squeeze in along with full-time work and child care—my fear is often that I am giving my board duties short shrift. For me, it feels very important that our work together as a board is managed efficiently, so time away from my young kids is not wasted."

Meanwhile, about 25 percent of survey respondents mentioned that they are retired or that their board is largely comprised of retirees. When asked about the time commitment required, many retired participants acknowledged that they have more time than board members who are in the workforce. Managing the expectations of how much time each person can dedicate to board work may make it easier for those with full-time jobs or young children to be involved.

Several studies have revealed that most membership organizations use the "engagement path" that appeals to Baby Boomers, which typically involves "lengthy periods of service on a board or committee." But this might not work as well for the younger generations.[4] According to Peggy M. Hoffman, president and association manager for Mariner Management, what Millennials and other younger volunteers want instead is to do "meaningful, mission-related activities . . . and then go home."[5]

How Younger Generations Are *Not* Different

We discovered early on that there were plenty of misconceptions about why various generations became involved with volunteering for the library. Younger board members, more so than their baby boomer counterparts, were seen as sharks circling for résumé fodder.

Our data, however, showed that across the generations, people became involved with library volunteer groups for the same reasons:

1. To be involved with their community. One survey respondent from a rural area said: "I feel that the library is vital to the success of citizens of the county."
2. Love of libraries and reading. "I love my library and wanted to support it."
3. They currently work (or have worked) in libraries. Respondents would mention working for academic libraries or in neighboring communities and wanting to help their residential library as well.
4. As a way to make a difference. One survey respondent said: "There were institutional troubles which I felt I had the skills and knowledge to help resolve."[6]

The one reason that showed up on the millennial list much more frequently was their children. One respondent said: "I wanted to make sure [our library] stays current and updated for young families."[7] At the time of surveying, Millennials were the generation most likely to have young children, though older generations also mentioned first getting reacquainted with the library "years ago" when their children were born. As such, the frequency of this response from Millennials was not a generational difference, but rather a representation of where the generational timeline is at the time of surveying. If we had surveyed 15 years ago, it would be Generation X. If we survey 15 years from now, it will be Generation Z.

NOTES

1. Lina Bertinelli, Madeline Jarvis, Kathy Kosinski, and Tess Wilson, "Beyond Using the Library: Engaging Millennials as Civic Library Leaders" (poster presented at the American Library Association Annual Conference, New Orleans, LA, June 2018), https://drive.google.com/file/d/1AdqBPpJowmHSLOUzvsXnbc0zG2jSr-Ek/view.
2. Genevieve Diesing, "Bringing Millennials on Board: The Transfer of Demographic Influence to the Millennial Generation May Change How Boards Operate," *Trustee* 11 (November/December 2016).
3. Corporation for National and Community Service, Volunteering in America, "Demographics," www.nationalservice.gov/serve/via/demographics.
4. John Barnes et al., *Exploring the Future of Membership* (Washington, DC: ASAE Foundation Research, 2014).
5. Marilyn Cavicchia, "Service in Small Bites: Microvolunteering and Member Engagement," *Bar Leader* 40, no. 5 (May-June 2016), www.americanbar.org/groups/bar_services/publications/bar_leader/2015-16/may-june/service-in-small-bites-microvolunteering-and-member-engagement/.
6. Bertinelli et al., "Beyond Using the Library."
7. Bertinelli et al., "Beyond Using the Library."

The ABCs of Recruitment and Retention

DID YOU KNOW THAT 65 PERCENT OF ALL U.S. FIREFIGHTERS ARE VOLUNteers? In fact, 65 percent of all fire departments in the United States are staffed solely by volunteers, with another 26 percent using some sort of volunteer staffing in their roster.[1] Only 9 percent of fire departments are staffed entirely by career, paid firemen. These numbers are surprising, and as you can expect, volunteer recruitment and retention are very important for fire departments because poor results can have dire consequences with regard to fire safety. A desperate library board member, foundation chair, or Friends group president may ask: how can we recruit like the firefighters? Many of the tips espoused in *Fire Engineering*'s "Volunteers Corner" can be boiled down to the "ABCs," or accessibility, buy-in, and confidence.[2]

ACCESSIBILITY: Improve access. Your organization needs to be easy to join and easy to understand.

BUY-IN: Gain buy-in from potential and new members by focusing on what they can achieve with your organization.

CONFIDENCE: Build confidence through providing training and support so that members stay engaged with their work and are able to grow their skill sets.

Recruitment Guidelines Brainstorm

It's as simple as 1-2-3! Take a personal look at your organization and list ways the Recruitment ABCs can be a communication tool.

ACCESSIBILITY
Improve access. Your organization needs to be easy to join and easy to understand.

Write down three places you can go (online or in person) to recruit new members:

1.

2.

3.

Write down three essential goals of your organization:

1.

2.

3.

BUY-IN
Gain buy-in from potential and new members by focusing on what they can achieve with your organization.

Write down three ways being involved in your organization has supported your professional and personal goals:

1.

2.

3.

CONFIDENCE
Build confidence through providing training and support so that members stay engaged with their work and are able to grow their skill sets.

Write down three ways you have been empowered or have helped empower others in your organization:

1.

2.

3.

Accessibility

Accessibility breaks down into two facets: easy to join and easy to understand. To recruit a successful and diverse membership on your board, Friends group, or foundation, you need to achieve both of these aims.

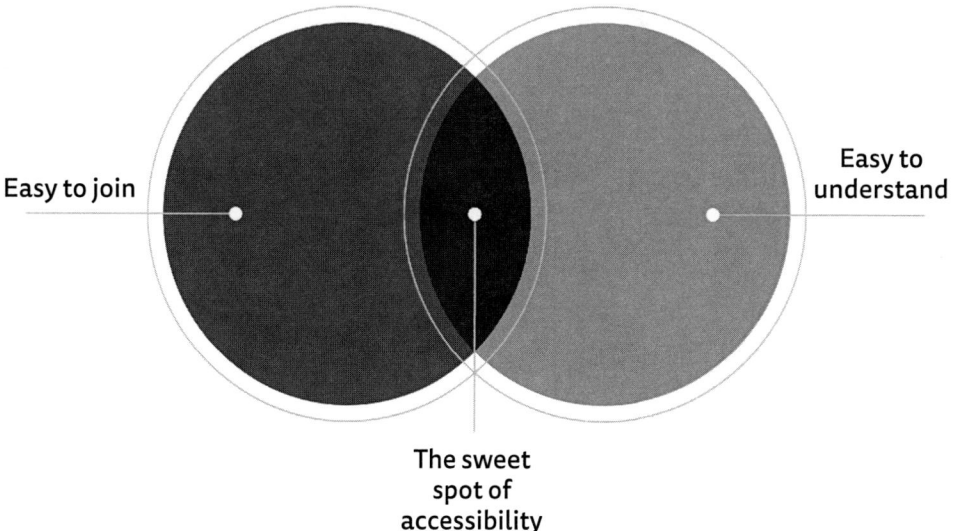

EASY TO JOIN

When recruiting for volunteer firefighters, firehouse staff warn against becoming a "Secret Society," and this is something that library groups can learn from.[3] The more open and inviting your group becomes to the community, the more likely you are to attract new members.

One firehouse recommends embracing social media with quick, hype-building videos that illustrate the type of work your group can do.[4] What are some of the impacts your group is making on your library? What are some of the amazing things you have been able to do with the capital you have raised? The video should inspire viewers to see your advocacy group as their way to make a measurable difference in the world. If you can rouse enthusiasm about the great things you are doing, you will also drive up volunteer numbers.

Accessibility also means starting young with outreach. Some firehouses create relationships with high schools that go "beyond an annual visit."[5] If you create a monthly, service-oriented club for your local students, they will be able to earn credits toward graduation while gaining valuable experience with your organization. One firehouse claims that its "high school service learning program has proven to be another vehicle that drives young volunteers to [the firehouse]." Getting high school students involved, especially in roles they can grow into, is a good way to turn the high turnover of high school students who volunteer into a smaller, yet still substantial pool of ongoing participants. With many high schools requiring volunteer service for graduation honors, a partnership can be a mutually beneficial relationship.

The Key to Ensuring Recruitment Success

Ask them. In our survey of 866 library trustees, Friends, and foundation members, we asked them how they were recruited to their board. Overwhelmingly, people told us that they were asked directly to participate:[6]

Generation	Percentage who were asked to participate
Silent Generation	63%
Baby Boomers	62%
Generation X	62%
Millennials	46%

Firehouses and nonprofits agree that the best way to recruit is to have current members do the asking.[7] People want to be liked, and they want to help. Asking people directly to participate in your group is the best way to get new members. Get in the habit of asking people to attend meetings or volunteer at the next event; make an effort to reach out to people of all ages and types.

EASY TO UNDERSTAND

People need to understand:

1. That you exist.
2. What you do.

This isn't something that fire departments need to undertake; people know they put out fires. This is an extra step that library organizations need to take. Once members become deeply involved in a library advocacy group, it can be difficult for them to recall a time when the group's purpose wasn't so clear-cut to them. But that purpose might not be nearly so obvious to potential volunteers and to the general public.

To give you an idea of this, think about a time when you had to teach someone how to drive. It might have been nerve-wracking—not only because you had an utter lack of control over the situation, but because everything that makes complete and total sense to you was incredibly difficult to put into words. Amount of pressure on the gas pedal? "I just know." When to shift gears? "When you reach this speed, shift into the next gear." Is there enough space to parallel park your car? "Looks like it." You were the expert and had all of this knowledge that was just second nature to you at that point. But communicating this knowledge to someone who has never driven a car before is difficult, weird, and new. Similarly, everyone reading this book, we assume, understands what a Friends group, a trustee board, or a foundation does for a library. It's easy to forget that not everyone in your community has your knowledge—that new members may be the equivalent of a teen driver: lost, confused, and trying their best to understand. You need to be able to make sure that both your veteran and your newest members (and in a best-case scenario, any community members) can easily describe what your group does in easy-to-understand terms.

One writer for *Fire Engineering*, Richard Ray, recommends writing a vision statement.[8] The benefits of a vision statement are twofold: people will know what your group does, and a good statement will inspire new members to join. Corporate or organizational vision statements vary in length, but an elevator pitch is shorter and is both more effective and easier to remember.

Adaptable Elevator Pitch Template

Elevator pitches are a succinct and sincere summary—short enough to be delivered during an average elevator ride. This exercise will help your volunteers be advocates, whether chatting in an elevator or catching up in a grocery checkout lane.

> (Group name)'s fundamental role is to (action/purpose) that (impact to community). Since (date/inception) we have (goals). As a result, we (accomplishment) including (specific example 1), (specific example 2), and (specific example 3). In the future, we will (specific example 4).

You can adjust the complexity and depth of the elevator pitch by changing the words surrounding the building blocks in the example above. The following are two sample elevator pitches tailored for different audiences.

"Dressed to Impress" Pitch

This elevator pitch is one that could work with an audience of city council members, potential donors, and other municipal officials:

> "The Friends of Smithtown Library's fundamental role is to provide financial, political, and cultural help to the library that will support an educated and safe community. Since 1981, we have helped the library afford new materials to create great experiences for the community. As a result, the Smithtown Library has a reputation for creative, accessible, and cutting-edge activities, including the state's largest community butterfly garden, STEAM craft kits available for checkout, and Braille-enhanced StoryWalks through Smithtown. In the future we are looking to build outreach with the senior community through library-hosted meals."

"Casual Friday" Pitch

If you're just trying to spread the word about your efforts without needing to impress people, you can scale it down with more casual language:

> "The Friends group's role is to help the library do all the cool things it can't do on its own. We've been around since the 1980s, and we've made Smithtown into one of the best libraries in the state. You know the butterfly garden? Those cool STEAM craft kits? That StoryWalk over there? That was all done with our help! Next we are going to try and reduce loneliness in the senior community by hosting regular meals at the library."

Now You Try It

(Group name) _____'s fundamental role is to (action/purpose) _____

_____

that (impact to community) _____

_____.

Since (date/inception) _____ we have (goals) _____

_____.

As a result, we (accomplishment) _____

_____,

including (specific example 1) _____,

(specific example 2) _____,

and (specific example 3) _____.

In the future, we will (specific example 4) _____

_____.

Go for the No

The word *no* only has as much power as we give it. Reach out to potential volunteers and run toward the *no*—create a board challenge as to who can collect the most refusals before the next meeting. Then analyze why you are getting *no's*—have you fine-tuned your elevator speech? Is your ask specific enough? Is it the right role for the right person?

You'll get plenty of "sure," "heck yes," and "why not?" answers along the way. Be sure to reward the board member who collects the most responses (for analysis) with a drink or a treat after your next meeting.

Pass out copies of the "No Log" at your next board meeting. Encourage your members to invite potential volunteers. Discuss reasons recruits may originally say "no" to think of solutions.

My No Log

Person	Reason for Refusal	Date

Buy-In

In order to retain new members, you need to make sure that you have buy-in from two groups: current organization members and your new recruits. Without simultaneous buy-in from both these groups, you can end up with infighting and conflicting factions. Firehouses are a good place to turn to for ideas. While you aren't generating buy-in for your volunteers and board members to rush into a burning building, the basic tenets that firemen use are still applicable. Fire Chief Dan Miller breaks buy-in into two stages, indoctrination and acceptance.[9] For our purposes, we will use the word *enthusiasm* instead of *indoctrination*. With enthusiasm and acceptance in place, you will have engaged organization members.

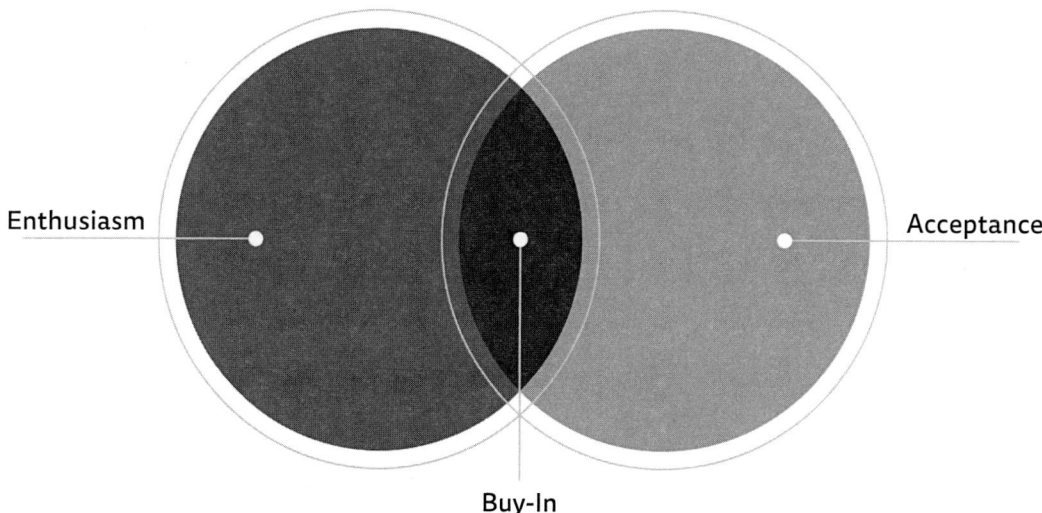

Additionally, as you consider how to build enthusiasm and acceptance in your organization, Fire Chief Tim Doran has a great quotation to keep in mind: "If the message is not about the listener, he is not listening. What's in it for him?"[10] Looking back to the previous chapter, you will remember that in the case of library organizations, "what's in it" for volunteers is the key reason that they joined in the first place: to make a difference.

ENTHUSIASM

Your new members need to be as excited about the group and its mission as the veterans are. They should be able to see "what's in it for them" quite easily. They should know your elevator pitch and they should know *directly* how they can fit into that elevator pitch. They should be able to see where they fit into the vision statement you have.

Building enthusiasm also means designing and advertising roles and tasks that reinforce both the organization's and the volunteers' goals. You can do this either proactively or reactively. Doing it proactively means creating position descriptions for the different volunteering tasks you need accomplished. By doing this, you will attract self-selecting volunteers who are interested in that specific type of work. Reactively, if one of your volunteers wants to increase their skills in a certain area, look for ways in which they can do so. For example, let's say your volunteer wants to learn Photoshop, and you have a project that needs someone to create advertising, invitations, and so on. This is a great opportunity to combine the two goals (personal and organizational) into something that is mutually beneficial.

Fire departments shared that after "organizational drama," "wasting time" had the most discouraging effect on volunteers staying active.[11] This means that if they aren't gaining personally, or they don't see how their work directly relates back to the elevator pitch of "making a difference," they may see working for your organization as a "waste of time," and no one wants that. One fire chief mentions that being "undertrained and underused" will result in "new members leaving for something more connected and fulfilling, with higher expectations and faster results."[12]

Minimizing Attrition

Fire Chief Miller came up with a list of ways to challenge new members for personal growth, while minimizing attrition.[13] While these procedures generally apply to firehouses, with a bit of creativity they can also work for your organization.

1. **Create training cohorts with a "rock-solid" start date. First, create a regimented training so that everyone goes through the same training.**
   Use a "rock-solid" start date to set expectations for a functioning group that members will know to hold true. A training cohort is a great way to create connections between members at the same time, so they have each other to look to if it is too intimidating to look to the veterans.

2. **Establish a lead instructor/mentor/training for the cohort.**
   Essentially, you want one person the trainees know they can go to who will answer their questions and help them.

3. **Establish standard operating procedures, and stick to them.**
   If you say the meeting starts at 6:00, don't start it at 6:20. It's about showing that their time matters, but your time matters too.

4. **Make sure that 70 percent of meeting time is used for hands-on skills practice.**
   This may not be a number your organization can reach, but it is an admirable goal to keep in mind. Is there anything you can physically do as a group during meetings? At the Library of Michigan, the highest-rated workshops for library staff are typically ones in which the staff get hands-on training for what they can do in the field.

5. **Expect high performance, but work with those who struggle.**
   Don't allow sloppy work to slide. Expect people to arrive on time, and let them know if they aren't meeting standards. If it seems they aren't making an effort, don't be afraid to let them go. If they are making an effort and it just doesn't seem to be working out, don't be afraid to put in a little extra effort coaching them. Multiple articles mention that some of the best and most committed volunteer firefighters are those who struggled and needed extra encouragement at the beginning.

6. **Finally, throw a graduation party at the end of training.**
   Instead of this, maybe you can just hold a recognition ceremony at a meeting or at an annual event you have. Something that lets the new members know that you appreciate all the hard work they have put in and will put in.

With these steps, Fire Chief Miller says that he loses 10 percent of his recruits in the first two weeks of his training academy, but he rarely loses anyone else after that. Most firehouses tend to lose 30–35 percent of their initial recruits, so he is looking at a pretty good record here. How does your volunteer retention rate compare to his?

ACCEPTANCE

If you find yourself making changes to your group in order to become more accessible and open to your whole community, you may have difficulty with some of the veteran volunteers who preferred how things have "always been done." In order not to lose their buy-in, and to maximize buy-in all the way round, you can benefit from a 2015 study that says:

> Analyses from 708 private-sector organizations found that the introduction of diversity training programs was associated with a *decrease* in the number of Black women in management (Kalev et al. 2006). One key to *minimizing such resistance and increasing support* for organizational diversity efforts among majority group members is to ensure that multiculturalism is framed inclusively, *highlighting the benefits* for both minority and majority group members.[14] (emphasis added)

Essentially, the study tells us that the way to get the most buy-in, and acceptance from both majority and minority groups, is to focus on how *everyone* will benefit. Once again, "what's in it for me?" An additional plan to help avoid creating an "old guard" and a "new guard" is to create a mentorship program. By working together through the "Know-Wonder-Learn Chart" (on the following page) and the "Board Member Orientation Checklist" (later in this book), a mentor and mentee can help build bridges and illustrate commonalities.

 Know-Wonder-Learn Chart

New board members may not know much about board life, or they may be experts on the subject. In order to help them organize their thoughts and knowledge, a Know-Wonder-Learn Chart can work wonders when delving into a new (or old) topic area. You should include these charts in your board trainee packets, and be sure to give new members time to work on them. The first two questions are to be completed at the beginning of orientation, while the "Learn" question is a great time for reflection when the orientation period is over.

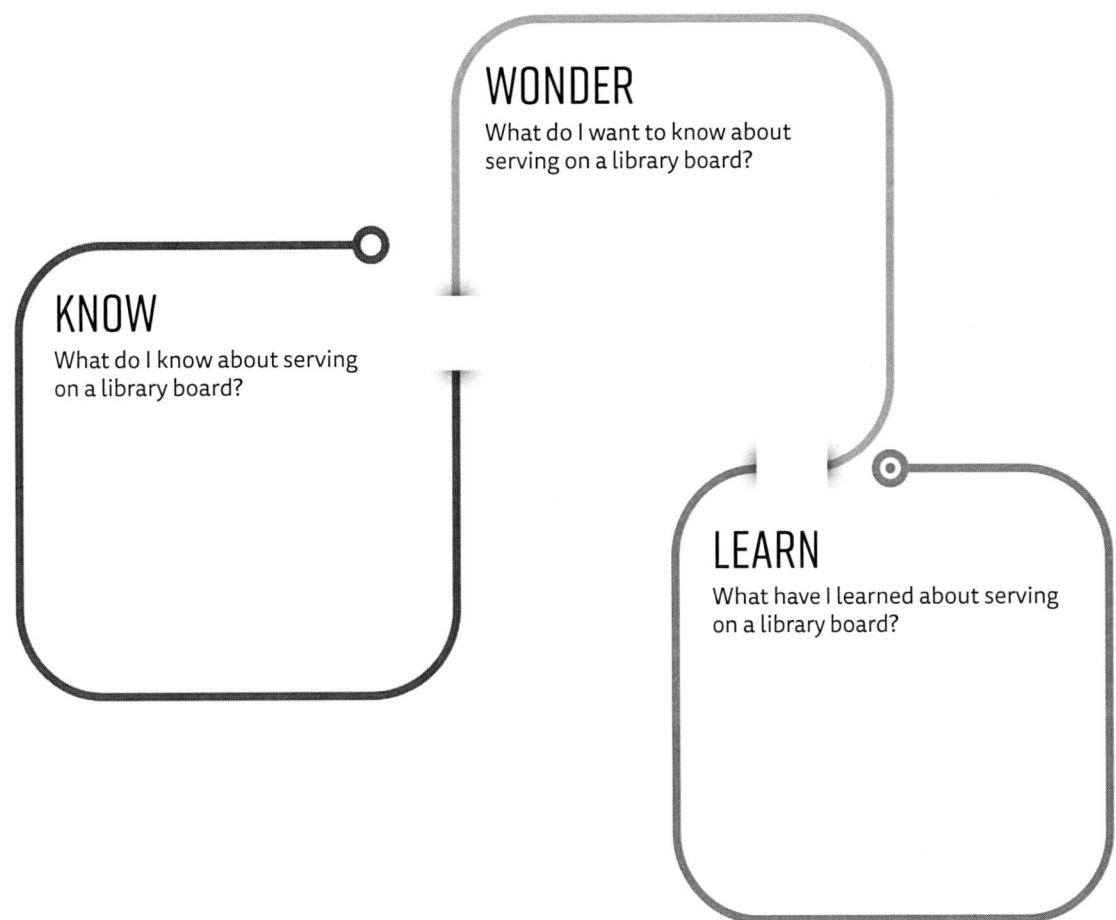

What's in It for Me?

When recruiting new members to your board, Friends group, or foundation, be prepared to sell them on the benefits of their involvement in it. Below are some common goals that people have when joining library groups and other volunteer activities. What are some specific ways your organization can help ensure that those goals are realized?

Goal	How Your Organization Can Help
To be involved in the community	
To fix a problem in the organization	
To improve the library for my children	
To support literacy initiatives	
To expand my network	
To develop my skills (leadership, fundraising, organizational)	
Fill in your own: What other benefits can your organization provide?	
Ask them: "What else is important to you?"	

What's in It for Me? Addressing Concerns

Potential members may understand the benefits of joining your group, but still hesitate to join. Maybe they had a disappointing experience in some other volunteer group or nonprofit board. What are some specific steps your organization is taking to alleviate these concerns?

Concern	Ways Your Organization Is Eliminating It
Inefficient meetings	
Inconvenient schedules	
Lack of diversity	
Not having a voice	
Ask them: "What concerns do you have?"	

Confidence

Once you have attracted new volunteers to your library group, you also need to make sure that they stay engaged and involved. Volunteering competes "with work, home, hobbies, children, church, and other community activities for volunteers' limited time."[15] In order to succeed against these competing interests, every single firehouse tries to support volunteers in a way that builds mutual confidence. This confidence, they argue, is the key to the retention of volunteers. "Teach, coach, recognize, and—most importantly—empower" is what Fire Chief Brian Berry suggests to recruiters.[16] Treating volunteers as professionals increases their enthusiasm and engagement: "Firefighters want to know that others in their department—especially leaders—trust them to do their job."[17] Excessive supervision and micromanaging will erode mutual trust and will chip away at your pool of available volunteers.

Your volunteers need to understand who the "point people" are for areas such as finance, marketing, and so on. Additionally, there also need to be ongoing trainings, mentorship, refresher courses, and other ways for them to retain and grow their skills. Fire Chief Miller mentions that in many firehouses without a good support system, it can take 3.5 years for volunteers to gain both confidence and buy-in. "This is a long time to wait and, frequently, it results in attrition of new members."[18] By doing everything you can to get volunteers feeling confident sooner, you will do a lot to keep members coming back. Giving your members the opportunity to develop additional professional skills, or the ability to flex the ones they already have, will often reinforce why they joined in the first place.[19]

 New Year's Reflection and Resolutions

The end of the year is the perfect time to reflect on what's going well, what could be improved on, what everyone has learned, and what questions still need to be answered. You can assess and create goals for the organization as a whole, but each member of your group should make individual reflections and resolutions as well. This activity can be completed at the end of the calendar year, fiscal year, or you can follow your term schedule.

This Year

I learned . . .

_____
_____
_____
_____

I reached out to . . .

_____
_____
_____
_____

I struggled with . . .

_____
_____
_____
_____

I am proud of . . .

_____
_____
_____
_____

Next Year

I will strengthen my understanding of . . .
_____
_____
_____
_____

I will accomplish this by . . .
_____
_____
_____
_____
_____

I will develop stronger relationships with . . .
_____
_____
_____
_____
_____

I will accomplish this by . . .
_____
_____
_____
_____

My priorities will be . . .
_____
_____
_____
_____

The 3-3-3 Rule

Every year, each board member should:

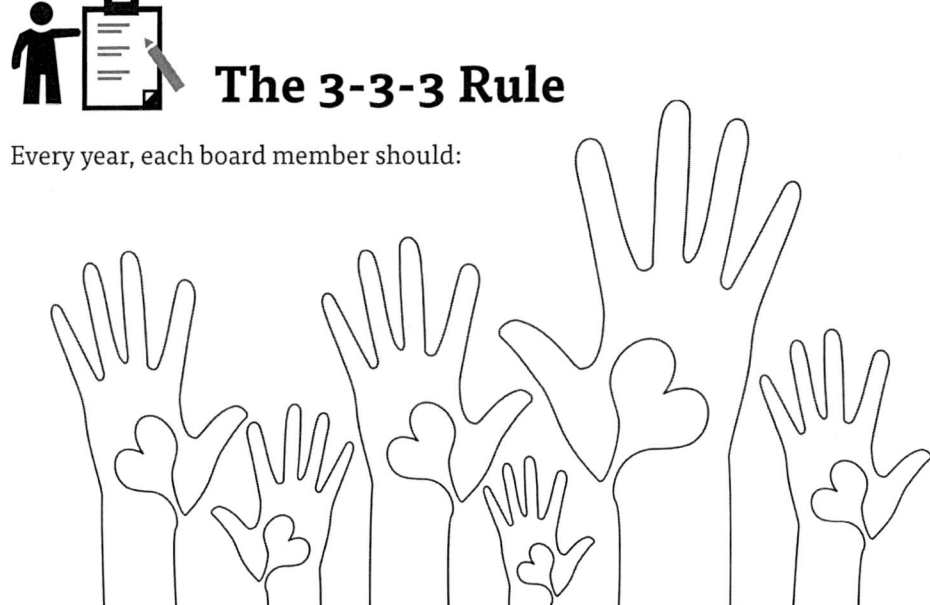

- **Contribute to your organization so it is one of their top three recipients of charitable donations.**
  Not everyone in your organization will be able to contribute the same amount of financial support, but everyone can make the organization a priority.

- **Introduce three new people or agencies to your organization.**
  Your members are ambassadors for the library and your advocacy group. Everyone should be comfortable bragging about the value of the library and the impact your group makes.

- **Attend three non-board-related events or activities at the library.** Your members should be library power users! Attending events will strengthen their understanding and connection to the library they're supporting. Encourage them to take their kids to a storytime, attend an author event, or learn a new skill at a workshop.

NOTES

1. Ben Evarts and Gary P. Stein, "U.S. Fire Department Profile 2017," National Fire Protection Association, March 2019, www.nfpa.org/News-and-Research/Data-research-and-tools/Emergency-Responders/US-fire-department-profile.
2. Scott Blue, "Reviving Your Volunteer Program," *Fire Engineering* 169, no. 3 (2016): 14–16.
3. Blue, "Reviving Your Volunteer Program."
4. Brian Berry, "Recruiting and Retaining Members," *Fire Engineering* 169, no. 4 (2016): 14–16.
5. Leza Raffel, "Targeted Recruitment Strategy Yields a Strong, Stable Membership," *Fire Engineering* 168, no. 8 (2015): 14–18.
6. Lina Bertinelli, Madeline Jarvis, Kathy Kosinski, and Tess Wilson, "Beyond Using the Library: Engaging Millennials as Civic Library Leaders" (poster presented at the American Library Association Annual Conference, New Orleans, LA, June 2018), https://drive.google.com/file/d/1AdqBPpJowmHSLOUzvsXnbc0zG2jSr-Ek/view.

7. Bertinelli et al., "Beyond Using the Library"; Evelyn Beck, "Why Don't People Volunteer?" PTO Today, December 9, 2015, www.ptotoday.com/pto-today-articles/article/5940-why-dont-people-volunteer.

8. Richard Ray, "Volunteer Departments: Winning on the Fireground," *Fire Engineering* 172, no. 7 (2019): 12–15.

9. Dan Miller, "Volunteer Academies: Change Outcomes by Challenging New Members," *Fire Engineering* 172, no. 6 (2019): 12–17.

10. Tim Doran, "They Voted Us Down: Push Back by Increasing Your Community Visibility," *Fire Engineering* 172, no. 1 (2019): 12–18.

11. John M. Buckman III, "Recruiting and Retaining Volunteers in 2019," *Fire Engineering* 172, no. 3 (2019): 12–14.

12. Miller, "Volunteer Academies."

13. Miller, "Volunteer Academies."

14. Adam D. Galinsky et al., "Maximizing the Gains and Minimizing the Pains of Diversity," *Perspectives on Psychological Science* 10, no. 6 (2015): 742–48, doi:10.1177/1745691615598513.

15. Raffel, "Targeted Recruitment Strategy."

16. Berry, "Recruiting and Retaining Members."

17. Ed Geis, "Rethinking Recruitment and Retention for Volunteer Fire Departments," *Fire Engineering* 168, no. 4 (2015): 12–13.

18. Miller, "Volunteer Academies."

19. Beck, "Why Don't People Volunteer?"

Defining and Managing Diversity for Your Advocacy Group

> Decades of research by organizational scientists, psychologists, sociologists, economists and demographers show that socially diverse groups (that is, those with a diversity of race, ethnicity, gender and sexual orientation) are more innovative than homogenous groups.
>
> —Katherine W. Phillips, *Scientific American*

DEFINING DIVERSITY IS A GOOD EXERCISE TO RETURN TO EVERY FEW years with your board, foundation, or Friends group. It can be beneficial to examine how your group sees diversity and whether you measure up to the goals you set. In the quotation above, Katherine Phillips lists the principal types of diversity: race, ethnicity, gender, and sexual orientation. Any definition of diversity for your advocacy group should begin with these types, but it is also useful to dig deeper.

You should explore the U.S. census data for your community.[1] Ask yourself, how does the makeup of our organization compare to the demographic makeup of our community? Does our population of volunteers mirror the community's makeup? Look for

- Race
- Ethnicity
- Gender
- Sexual Orientation
- Income
- Disability
- Age
- Education
- Language
- Military Veteran

Actively looking for and recruiting diverse volunteers benefits everyone. Diversity (whether in groups or even within an individual's experiences) produces better decisions and more innovation for all involved.[2] Simply put: "Being around people who are different from us makes us more creative, more diligent, and harder-working."[3]

It is important to try to increase the diversity of your membership with sincerity and not simply as a way to check off representation boxes. As one United for Libraries survey respondent said, "cycling through a token person is not impactful," and can instead have negative consequences for both the volunteer and the group.[4] Transparency about your recruitment aims will aid your efforts: many underrepresented demographics will often decline to volunteer for organizations that seem "unwelcoming."[5] Transparency is also best done through a multicultural lens. Include language in your recruitment efforts that emphasizes the equitable, diverse, and open atmosphere of your Friends group. Including specific words, such as *equity* and *inclusivity*, can signal to minority groups that your organization is a friendly place without arousing resistance from a majority group that may view the recruitment effort as exclusionary.[6]

United for Libraries has many resources available for building equity, diversity, and inclusion into your library advocacy efforts. The board assessment activities included in this book have been adapted from "A Library Board's Practical Guide to Board Self Evaluation." You can find this resource in full, as well as many others, at www.ala.org/united.

NOTES

1. U.S. Census Bureau, "American FactFinder," https://factfinder.census.gov/faces/nav/jsf/pages/index.xhtml.
2. Adam D. Galinsky et al., "Maximizing the Gains and Minimizing the Pains of Diversity," *Perspectives on Psychological Science* 10, no. 6 (2015): 742–48, doi:10.1177/1745691615598513.
3. Katherine W. Phillips, "How Diversity Works," *Scientific American* 311, no. 4 (2014): 43–47, doi:10.1038/scientificamerican1014-42.
4. Lina Bertinelli, Madeline Jarvis, Kathy Kosinski, and Tess Wilson, "Beyond Using the Library: Engaging Millennials as Civic Library Leaders" (poster presented at the American Library Association Annual Conference, New Orleans, LA, June 2018), https://drive.google.com/file/d/1AdqBPpJowmHSLOUzvsXnbc0zG2jSr-Ek/view.
5. Galinsky et al., "Maximizing the Gains and Minimizing the Pains of Diversity."
6. Galinsky et al., "Maximizing the Gains and Minimizing the Pains of Diversity."

Onboarding: Tried and True Practices

I N 1979 TEM HORWITZ PRESENTED THE PAPER "LEADERSHIP DYNAMICS AND the Governing Board of a Library Friends Group" at the Allerton Park Institute. His suggested goals for boards remain true:

1. The board members should be effective individually in their work.
2. They should have complementary talents.
3. They should be representative of the interests served by the organization.
4. The board should be large enough to get all the work done, but small enough to be intimate.
5. There should be clear organizational patterns and good communication between the board and the library staff.
6. It is essential to have good working relationships among the board, the staff, and the organization's executive.
7. The board should have a total sense of the organization's objectives.
8. The board should know to what degree these objectives are being realized by the organization.
9. The members should be comfortable with one another.
10. Each member should feel involved with the work of the board and the progress of the organization.
11. The board should have specific goals.
12. The board should make policy decisions only after talking to all concerned parties; it should not operate in a vacuum.
13. The board should enjoy good relationships with the community.
14. Members should derive a sense of achievement from their board work.[1]

Volunteering is a two-way street; volunteers should expect clear guidelines and meaningful engagement from their service, and volunteer agencies should expect focused and dedicated work. Regarding volunteer roles in the same light as a job helps provide the focus and framework needed for successful engagement. You should respect your potential volunteers' expertise and provide opportunities for their skill sets to shine if aligned with the library's mission.

When recruiting volunteers, you should "use an intake process consisting of a job description, application, and interview."[2] The job description can be as simple as a list of common tasks and goals paired with an average monthly time commitment. An interview provides a potential volunteer with the opportunity to get to know the organization as well. If the two parties decide it's a good fit, they can move forward with an orientation to your group. The orientation does not need to be exhaustive, but rather just the tools and tricks needed to contribute to board meetings.

Within the orientation, you should include information about general library services. You can partner with a staff member who is excited about upcoming initiatives for a special welcome, or ask a training lead what onboarding new library staff should receive. For a general orientation on library services, check with your state library for suggested resources for volunteer boards. If your board is completely revamping the orientation process, you should allow current members to undergo the orientation in order to renew their understanding and appreciation of twenty-first-century library services. A 2018 United for Libraries survey participant saw in their board of trustees "a gap in generational attitudes about library policies—for example, around standards of professionalism for library employees, whether that's things like personal appearance, etiquette, etc. For people out of the workforce for a while, I think there's also a disconnect around budget, benefits, and salary issues—I have had numerous board members who think they should be able to get a great candidate for a professional job requiring an MLS for $30K. Because in their life experience, 'that's a decent salary.' They need to be at the table too, because they represent a lot of folks in the community struggling to live on a fixed income.... Different generational perspectives around the table when looking at these kinds of things are so critical."[3] As a fundraising nonprofit designed to supplement the library's budget, it is imperative to know where the representational gaps are and which projects could best propel the library's mission.

When defining roles for your advocacy group beyond the executive committee, think about the work that needs to be done to ensure your group's success. Using task forces rather than committees can help your group focus on special projects, such as specific events or single initiatives, and will help provide opportunities for potential volunteers with busy schedules to give back to their community.

You should set and respect board term limits. One survey respondent explained it as "Too long, people take over and forget they are a team. Too short, and they miss board training or don't find their niche."[4] The majority of boards employ renewable three-year terms.

If you hope that young members will be your sole source of book sale support, be strategic and authentic in your recruitment for that specific task. A Friends board member who responded to the United for Libraries survey had a great volunteer pool for set-up: "We have a carpenters' union helping us with the Book Sales. They lift heavy boxes of books and place them adjacent to appropriate areas for volunteers to unpack. Then post-sale, they load a truck to take away the remainders."[5]

When working with others who are passionate about your community, it's easy for meetings and social hours to blur together. Consider adding an optional social hour outside of the regularly scheduled meetings in order to keep connections and camaraderie fresh. Meetings seen as inefficient are often the "kiss of death" for young parents and early professionals.[6] Keep your meetings focused on work in order to be respectful of participants' time, and collaborate on completing action items prior to the meetings. About 93 percent of respondents to the 2018 United for Libraries survey said they prefer e-mail communication between meetings.

Forty years later, and the guidelines presented by Tem Horwitz remain true.

Circles of Influence Activity

Your volunteer service is making a difference in your community. Help your organization by giving others the chance to be a part of this vital work. Pass out copies of this worksheet at your next board meeting, and ask each member to take ten minutes to scroll through their phone, e-mail, and social media contacts and then fill the sheet out. They should list the person's name and contact information on each blank line below. Next time you are looking to fill vacancies or create task forces, have your members take a look at the untapped resources in their own circles of influence.

People who have expressed interest in the library to me:

_____

_____

The doers in the community:

_____

_____

_____

Friends who follow technology trends:

_____

_____

_____

Parents who are looking to improve their kids' community:

_____

_____

_____

The last three people you've shared book recommendations with:

_____

_____

_____

Some of your pals at work:

_____

_____

_____

Look Around: Lessons Learned from Other Industries

Redefine Membership Status

You're a firefighter or an emergency medical services member—that's often the limit for real membership opportunities in the volunteer firehouse. That made sense when our houses were full and our jobs were much different. However, today's modern firehouse is a complex operation that requires a diverse team skill set. Who is your department's treasurer? Secretary? Photographer? Web master or social media manager? It is time to redefine membership and rethink volunteer opportunities in the fire service that not only fulfill our emergency response obligations, but also help manage and support our entire organization.

—Blaize Levitan, State of Connecticut Firefighter II

Are you asking your twentieth-century volunteer positions to deliver twenty-first-century results? **Challenge your board to reach out to four area nonprofits or volunteer boards and ask them how and whom they recruit for positions.** Maybe the food co-op or fire department in your community has redefined certain roles in order to achieve more dynamic results.

Group: _____

Recruitment wins: _____

_____

Recruitment challenges: _____

_____

Volunteer roles: _____

_____

Lessons learned: _____

_____

Group: _____

Recruitment wins: _____

_____

Recruitment challenges: _____

_____

Volunteer roles: _____

_____

Lessons learned: _____

_____

Group: _____

Recruitment wins: _____

_____

Recruitment challenges: _____

_____

Volunteer roles: _____

_____

Lessons learned: _____

_____

Group: _____

Recruitment wins: _____

_____

Recruitment challenges: _____

_____

Volunteer roles: _____

_____

Lessons learned: _____

_____

The Value of Mentoring

In addition to partnering with a staff member to become familiar with library practices, norms, and expectations, mentorship can be an integral part of understanding the culture of both the library and its board. Pairing a veteran board member with a new recruit is not only an incredibly effective way of integrating new members, but it also is a relationship ripe with opportunities for the mentor, the mentee, and the board at large:

- **Perspective.** Undoubtedly, the insights your experienced board members can offer will be of great importance to your new recruits, and the model of their behavior is invaluable. Mentees are simultaneously tasked with navigating the "learning landscape of the organization" and the board's direction, and a trusted guide is essential during this stage.[7] However, the mentor-mentee relationship is more often than not a two-way street. In this case, mentors should consider the benefits of bringing a fresh perspective into their boardroom. New recruits have the advantage of not knowing the nuances of your particular group, and this can be an opportunity for constructive conversations and possible reassessment of any practices or processes that have become second nature for veteran members.
- **Trust.** Being the newest member of an established group can be an intimidating and—if not approached through the lens of mentorship—disheartening experience. This is especially true if generational gaps exist within the group. The mentor-mentee space can provide warmth during this period of navigation. Mentors have a responsibility to establish this relationship as one in which both confusion and curiosity are welcome.
- **Accountability.** Of course, the mentor is not the only one with responsibilities in this relationship. Both mentee and mentor are expected to tackle duties as assigned and to continue working toward the larger goals of the board. Maintaining an open and consistent dialogue is essential for an effective mentorship, but it can also be a helpful accountability tool. Mentors and mentees should work together to set and renegotiate goals while encouraging and challenging each other.

Every library is different, as is the board that supports it. Each library and its board present a new landscape to navigate, with hills and valleys to consider and conquer. You, as a mentor, should serve as a trusted guide during this time. Have the new member work through the "Board Member Orientation Checklist" on the following page.

HOW TO USE THE CHECKLIST
- Print two copies of the checklist, one for the new board member (or mentee) and one for the board mentor.
- The mentee should check off the steps as she finishes them.
- The mentee should try to have the first section, "Getting Oriented," finished within the first 30 days. The other two sections should be finished within the first 60 days.

Board Member Orientation Checklist

Board Member Name: _____

Please complete all items on this checklist by _____/_____/_____.

If I have any questions, my Board Mentor is _____.

Getting Oriented

- ☐ Go on a full facility tour of the library building/s.
- ☐ Meet staff members.
- ☐ Meet your Board Mentor.
- ☐ Meet with the Board Chair and Library Director for an overview on the library's history, mission, and vision, including how the board and Director work within it all.
- ☐ Review the board orientation packet with the Board Mentor. This packet should contain:
  - ☐ List of current board members
  - ☐ Board meeting schedule/calendar
  - ☐ Calendar of upcoming library events
  - ☐ Friends of the Library information and roster
  - ☐ Library Foundation information and roster
  - ☐ Local cooperative information
  - ☐ The most recent Strategic Plan
  - ☐ Board member's role description
  - ☐ Library organizational chart
  - ☐ Library policy manual
  - ☐ Approved budget for the fiscal year
  - ☐ Most recent annual reports
  - ☐ State library information
  - ☐ United for Libraries' Public Library Trustee Ethics Statement
  - ☐ Open Meetings Act (if applicable)
  - ☐ Log-in information for United for Libraries (if applicable)

(continued)

Financial Matters
- ☐ Set a meeting with the Treasurer
- ☐ Review financial documentation
- ☐ Review the budget process
    - ☐ When it happens (fiscal year dates)
    - ☐ Who is involved in the budget?
    - ☐ Millage campaigns (if applicable)
- ☐ Review the funding sources
    - ☐ Millage campaigns
    - ☐ Cooperatives
    - ☐ State aid
    - ☐ Federal aid
    - ☐ Grants
    - ☐ Foundations/Friends groups
- ☐ Review the current fiscal budget

Board Operations
With your Board Mentor:
- ☐ Go over the minutes for the three previous board meetings.
- ☐ Review board meeting logistics.
    - ☐ When and where they are held
    - ☐ How the agenda is set
    - ☐ Open meetings/closed meetings
    - ☐ Digital attendance at meetings
- ☐ How your role fits within the board
- ☐ The board's relationship to the Library Director

Board Mentor Check-Ins
Meet with your Board Mentor periodically for check-ins:
- ☐ Check-in #1, in-person at one month: _____/_____/_____
- ☐ Check-in #2, in-person or by phone at three months: _____/_____/_____

Board Mentorship Worksheet —Mentor

Use this worksheet as often as you would like—at your initial orientation or for every meeting. Focus your conversation on the needs of the organization and mentee using the following questions as guides.

Today's date: _____   Next meeting: _____

Progress

What did you discuss during your last meeting? What has happened since?

_____
_____
_____
_____

Process

What does your mentee want help with? Do you fully understand their concerns and needs?

_____
_____
_____
_____

Plan

What needs to be done for your mentee to take on their latest project or problem with confidence?

_____
_____
_____
_____

What did you learn about your mentee today?

What will you follow up on at your next meeting?

What will you get done before your next meeting?

Board Mentorship Worksheet —Mentee

Use this worksheet as often as you would like—at your initial orientation or for every meeting. Focus your conversation on the needs of the organization and mentee using the following questions as guides.

Contribution

What is one accomplishment you can share? Did you just complete a project? What is your latest idea?

_____

_____

Conundrum

What is a problem you need help with? What challenges are you facing?

_____

_____

Curiosity

What is one question you still have?

_____

_____

What did you learn about your mentor today?

_____

_____

What will you follow up on at your next meeting?

_____

_____

What will you get done before your next meeting?

_____

_____

Board Mentorship One-Month Spark Igniter—Mentee

What EXCITES you about your group?

_____
_____

How can you ENERGIZE your group?

_____
_____

Board Mentorship Three-Month Spark Igniter—Mentee

What EXCITES you about your group?

_____
_____

How can we ENGAGE our community?

_____
_____

Board Mentorship Six-Month Spark Igniter—Mentee

What EXCITES you about your group?

_____
_____

What should we EXAMINE about our group?

_____
_____

NOTES

1. Tem Horwitz, "Leadership Dynamics and the Governing Board of a Library Friends Group" (paper presented at the Allerton Park Institute, November 11–14, 1979).
2. Kaitlin Throgmorton, "Recruiting and Retaining Volunteers," *American Libraries,* May 31, 2016, https://americanlibrariesmagazine.org/2016/05/31/recruiting-retaining-library-volunteers/.
3. Lina Bertinelli, Madeline Jarvis, Kathy Kosinski, and Tess Wilson, "Beyond Using the Library: Engaging Millennials as Civic Library Leaders" (poster presented at the American Library Association Annual Conference, New Orleans, LA, June 2018), https://drive.google.com/file/d/1AdqBPpJowmHSLOUzvsXnbc0zG2jSr-Ek/view.
4. Bertinelli et al., "Beyond Using the Library."
5. Bertinelli et al., "Beyond Using the Library."
6. Bertinelli et al., "Beyond Using the Library."
7. "Guidelines Assist Board Mentors," *Board & Administrator for Administrators Only* 36, no. S3 (2019): 9.

Fundraising with the Debt Generations

Although millennial survey respondents were excited by opportunities to donate their time and effort, raising funds from this "debt generation" poses unique challenges for nonprofits. Households headed by Millennials are more likely to be in poverty than households led by any other generation. Roughly 31 percent of all households living in poverty were headed by a Millennial as of 2016.[1] Additionally, 57 percent of Millennials describe student debt as a "major problem"; this is not surprising, given that the total outstanding student loan debt in the United States is more than $1.5 trillion.[2] For those who are essentially paying off a mortgage in the form of their student debt (and who doubt they will ever stop renting), an annual campaign or ticketed fundraiser event aimed at them may not be as successful an approach as it was with their parents and grandparents. The average donor in the United States is sixty-two years old, and the fundraising appeals that have worked with Baby Boomers do not always translate to a millennial audience.[3]

Ultimately, fundraising provides donors with the opportunity to support their own goals and dreams: "Donors want to know why they should give. And especially why they should give now. And why you have chosen them to make a gift. You, the dream weaver, must answer these questions" as Millennials decide where to donate their scarce resources.[4] As local dream weavers, we recommend that Friends and foundations pair fundraisers with their community's events, interests, and values.

Pair with Community Events or Local Identity

The following three case studies feature libraries of different sizes in different states. The tie that unites them is their celebration of their patrons and places. Think about your community as you review these events—what could be the most "you" FUNdraiser possible?

CASE STUDY: BOOK ACROSS THE BAY (WASHBURN, WI)

Some folks might pay money to not be outside on a lake on a freezing February night. That's not the case in Washburn, Wisconsin, where an annual 10-kilometer ski and snowshoe race across Lake Superior's Chequamegon Bay attracts thousands of racers and spectators every year. Book Across the Bay started in 1996 as a joint fundraiser for the Washburn Public Library and the Tri-County Medical Society. The race begins in nearby Ashland, and the course is lit by over 1,000 lights. A local resident explains: "The buzz starts well over a month before it happens: you can feel the pride in the community and the event. That buzz, that excitement, shifts to almost stress a few days ahead of it: the town's going to be busy."[5]

CASE STUDY: GET INKED FOR THE LIBRARY (LAWRENCE, KS)

Would you like a permanent declaration of your love for the library? For National Library Week 2019, the Lawrence Public Library Foundation partnered with Standard Electric Tattooing on a tattoo fundraiser. Tattoo artists Holly and Jarod Hackney created eight flash tattoos for the event. To respect the artists' time, no alterations were allowed to designs, and tattoos were only allowed on arms and legs. Participants were required to be 18+ and present a valid ID. The one-day fundraiser generated $4,000. Logan Isaman, the assistant to the Lawrence Public Library Foundation, was thrilled at the event's success and looks forward to repeating it in the future. What is on her list of things to keep in mind? Making sure the participants are not going in on an empty stomach, and that the artists are tipped fairly for their labor.[6]

CASE STUDY: LIBRARY LIBATIONS (RALEIGH, NC)

Storytimes are a great way for parents to meet and mingle, while book groups are the perfect setting for adults to chat with other readers. But Leia Droll of North Carolina State University (NCSU) Libraries asks, where can adult patrons "enjoy hors d'oeuvres and alcoholic beverages while learning more about the library's offerings" and feel free to explore the library in an intimate setting?[7] Increasingly, libraries are using alcoholic beverages to tap into their adult patron base in new, creative ways.

Through their Library Libations series, the NCSU Friends of the Library promotes a variety of library offerings, collections, and special-interest events to attendees. What sets these events apart from regularly scheduled programming, however, is the inclusion of drinks and hors d'oeuvres. Reportedly, this series has not only been quite popular with guests, but it has also "helped attract many younger alumni to the Friends group."[8]

Overall, this event serves as both a successful fundraiser and an effective marketing tool for the library.[9] But beyond that, it has also proven to be an inventive and sustainable way to attract younger members to the Friends group.

Think Outside the Box

Tap into local venues: Ask your local bar or brewery if they will donate their patrons' tips to your Friends organization for the night in exchange for volunteer labor as guest servers. This "fun" raiser helps you meet potential donors and members when they feel the most generous.

Don't wait, collaborate: Connect across your community—what about sponsoring a 5K race, a Bob Ross paint along, or a murder mystery party? Listen to your community and pay attention to the successful fundraisers that have been held in other nonprofit fields.

Make giving easy: Donations can go beyond cash or a handwritten check. Does your website link to a PayPal or Venmo? The retention rate for online donors is 58 percent for future gifts.[10]

Every penny matters: Even if your younger donors—whether Millennials, Gen Z, or younger—don't have the capacity to give a large gift, every gift matters. Even an annual $5.00 gift creates a culture of philanthropy that, when acknowledged and appreciated, will continue to grow through time.

Give, Get, Save: Members and Money

Board members and volunteers help maximize an organization's resources. Simply put, we help protect the library's bottom line. Are you best at helping to give money, get money, or save money? Take this quiz and find out:

1. There's a chili cookoff being planned for February. How are you most comfortable helping out?
    a. I'll do a grocery run the day before. You can never have enough napkins for events like this. I'm also going to drop off an extra donation as I sample the entries in order to help us reach our goal faster.
    b. I'm going to ask our local bakery to donate cornbread for the day. I'm excited about the event and look forward to helping others get involved in our work.
    c. Just call me the SignUp Genius guru. I'll get the logistics organized and break up volunteer needs into manageable two-hour chunks.

2. Your new neighbors mention they would like to check out the Friends' book sale next weekend. They are avid readers and love the library. How do you respond?
    a. I'll ask them if they would like to go to the Friends-only presale with me. Early-bird access is free for the low price of an annual Friends membership.
    b. I'll introduce them to some of the other volunteers as they shop at the book sale. Maybe they could help out with next year's sale and create display tables of impulse buys near the checkout table in order to help with funds.
    c. I'll let them know when I'll be volunteering and ask if they'd like to hang out with me at the table. It's a nice way to get to know a new friend, and the Sunday afternoon shift is usually pretty laid back.

3. How do you like to give back?
    a. I like to make room in my budget for the organizations and causes that mean the most to me and know that I'm helping out.
    b. I like to share news about the organizations and causes that mean the most to me and get others involved.
    c. I like to volunteer a few hours per month for the organizations and causes that mean the most to me and see the difference I can make.

Answers

IF YOU GOT MOSTLY As: GIVE MONEY

You have a heart of gold—giving back is in your nature. Whether buying books at the annual Friends book sale or writing a check to help the foundation reach an ambitious goal, the library is near and dear to you. Continue to give back and ask your library staff liaison which initiatives would have the biggest impact this year.

IF YOU GOT MOSTLY Bs: GET MONEY

You are great at leveraging connections and resources to improve your community. Your library needs more social butterflies like you to share its challenges and wins. Continue to connect the volunteers and donors in your social circle with the organization.

IF YOU GOT MOSTLY Cs: SAVE MONEY

Time is the greatest gift to share, and you give it in spades. Your resourcefulness and generosity actually save the library money: setting up tables and running the book sale will make shoppers' browsing experiences more enjoyable. You are paving the way for funds to come in simply through your "fun" work.

NOTES

1. Richard Fry, "5 Facts about Millennial Households," Pew Research Center, September 6, 2017, www.pewresearch.org/fact-tank/2017/09/06/5-facts-about-millennial-households/.
2. Nick Terzian, "Guidelines for Fundraising from Millennials," Whole Whale, 2019, www.wholewhale.com/tips/guidelines-fundraising-millennials/; Zack Friedman, "Student Loan Debt Statistics in 2019: A $1.5 Trillion Crisis," *Forbes,* February 25, 2019, www.forbes.com/sites/zackfriedman/2019/02/25/student-loan-debt-statistics-2019/#3e85e02a133f.
3. Terzian, "Guidelines for Fundraising from Millennials."
4. Jerrod Panas, *The Fundraising Measuring Stick: Sizing Up Attributes Board Members, Volunteers, and Staff Must Cultivate to Secure Major Gifts* (Medfield, MA: Emerson & Church, 2016).
5. Charles Jarvis, "Resident Perspective on Book Across the Bay," personal interview, 2019.
6. Logan Isaman, "Get Inked for Library Fundraiser," personal interview, 2019.
7. Anne Ford, "Libations in the Library," *American Libraries,* March 1, 2019, https://americanlibrariesmagazine.org/2019/03/01/libations-library-alcohol-friendly-events/.
8. Ford, "Libations in the Library."
9. NC State University Libraries, "Library Libations Series," www.lib.ncsu.edu/library-libations-series.
10. Terzian, "Guidelines for Fundraising from Millennials."

Conclusion
Assess, Adapt, Attract

ARTICLE AFTER ARTICLE DOCUMENTS AN INCREASING NUMBER OF MIL-lennials interacting with libraries. With reasons ranging from "appreciat[ing] free community spaces and in-person programming" to simply "lik[ing] the feeling the library gives me," this group is engaging with libraries in a wide variety of ways.[1] Just as some libraries have shifted their fundraising tactics to attract younger patrons, others are making more permanent, large-scale changes as a way to adapt to their patrons' changing needs.

In what was referred to as a "significant milestone" in its history, the Boston Public Library renovated its Central Library in 2015–16 with several notable forward-thinking changes, including

> removal of the granite plinths that covered the Johnson building windows, reconnecting the building to the street; a revamped lecture hall for author talks and programming, a new innovation center, new Mac and Windows computers for the public computing area, a hi-tech community learning center, an enlarged Fiction section and new ways of book browsing, digital stacks to explore the BPL's digitized collections, a state-of-the-art Welcome Center, [and] a digital imaging suite.[2]

Clearly, this is a library that has embraced and adapted to the technological, physical, and social needs of millennial patrons. It is essential for libraries to realize that changes like these can fortify existing relationships, solidify buy-in from an established group of the workforce, increase libraries' appeal to a wider swath of the public, and broaden their capacity to evolve with an ever-changing environment. It is equally essential for library interest groups to understand their role in this equation, and examine the mindsets, tendencies, and priorities of Millennials.

But these adaptations are not always brick-and-mortar ones, and they do not need to be fundamental shifts in operation or attitude. With this book, we hope your interest group will feel an increased sense of flexibility when it comes to working with and for your younger members. The issue of engaging, recruiting, and keeping young members is not likely to end with this book—nor, indeed, with this particular generation. But we hope this book arms you with a practical approach and a strong foundation for moving forward.

NOTES

1. Story Hinckley, "Libraries Obsolete? No Way, Say Millennials," *Christian Science Monitor*, August 14, 2017, www.csmonitor.com/USA/Society/2017/0814/Libraries-obsolete-No-way-say-Millennials.

2. City of Boston. "Boston Public Library Celebrates Central Library Renovation Opening." January 13, 2017. www.boston.gov/news/boston-public-library-celebrates-central-library-renovation-opening.

Additional Resources

Bilimoria, Diana, and Ruth Sessler Bernstein. "Diversity Perspectives and Minority Nonprofit Board Member Inclusion." *Equality, Diversity and Inclusion: An International Journal* 32, no. 7 (2013): 636–53.

Capoziello, Michael. "Creating Positive Public Relations." *Fire Engineering* 170, no. 2 (2017): 12–19.

Greene, David A. "The Declining Membership of the Volunteer Fire Service." *Fire Engineering* 172, no. 2 (2019): 12–15.

Haigh, Craig A. "Juggling Hats: Managing a Volunteer, Combination, or Small Career Department." *Fire Engineering* 172, no. 8 (2019): 33.

Hanks, Kathy. "A Sign of Permanent Devotion: People Pay $100 to Get a Tattoo, Support the Lawrence Public Library." *Lawrence Journal-World*, April 9, 2019. www2.ljworld.com/news/general-news/2019/apr/09/a-sign-of-permanent-devotion-people-pay-100-to-get-a-tattoo-support-the-lawrence-public-library/.

Hurst, Aaron, "Nonprofits Will Lose Workers to Business Unless They Feel a Sense of Purpose." *Chronicle of Philanthropy* 26, no. 10 (2014): 31–33.

Kim, Mirae, and Dyana P. Mason. "Representation and Diversity, Advocacy, and Nonprofit Arts Organizations." *Nonprofit and Voluntary Sector Quarterly* 47, no. 1 (2018): 49–71.

Levitan, Blaize. "Saving Volunteer Fire Service for the Next Generation." *Fire Engineering* 172, no. 11 (2019): 12–14.

Merrill, Thomas A. "Make It a Fire-HOUSE." *Fire Engineering* 170, no. 4 (2017): 14–18.

Shaw, Haydn. *Sticking Points: How to Get 4 Generations Working Together in the 12 Places They Come Apart*. Carol Stream, IL: Tyndale Momentum, 2013.

Testy, Kellye Y. "Best Practices for Hiring and Retaining a Diverse Law Faculty." *Iowa Law Review* 96, no. 5 (2011): 1707–18.

United for Libraries. www.ala.org/united.

Wallestad, Anne, Vernetta Walker, and Ruth McCambridge. "How to Address Your Nonprofit's Board Diversity." *The Nonprofit Quarterly*, 2017. YouTube video. www.youtube.com/watch?v=4AR1eRE-RIw&feature=youtu.be.

Wells, Devon. "Lead Your Rural Agency to Success with an Organizational Philosophy." *Fire Engineering* 171, no. 11 (2018): 12–13.

Interested in multiple copies for meetings or trainings?

Go to **alastore.ala.org/action-planner** to learn more about purchasing a cost-effective, downloadable, and print-ready PDF.

ALSO OF INTEREST

Proving Your Library's Value: Persuasive, Organized, and Memorable Messaging

A UNITED FOR LIBRARIES ACTION PLANNER

Alan Fishel and Jillian Wentworth
PRINT: 978-0-8389-4741-8

You know the value of your library, but elected officials, donors, community leaders, funders, and other important stakeholders may not. How can you make the library a priority for these groups, which may have preconceived notions about what the library does, as you compete with other important community organizations for funding? In this book from United for Libraries, you'll learn how to use The E's of Libraries® (Education, Employment, Entrepreneurship, Engagement, and Empowerment) to quickly demonstrate why your library is essential and worthy of funding, using messaging that is organized, persuasive, and memorable. With the help of worksheets, charts, and prompts, you will learn how to

- use language designed to win over stakeholders, funders, and partners;
- craft custom messaging in several formats that is easily accessible and memorable, including elevator speeches, budget presentations, and annual appeals; and
- create presentations and other materials tailored to any audience based on the sample documents included.

alastore.ala.org/action-planner